"Revitalizing our lives is needed today! The format of this interactive work encourages me to want to read this book, sharpen my focus, personally improve, and accept the blessing of daily revitalizing my life. The text is Godly, the action steps are open minded, and the power of God refreshing."

— **Thelma Wells,** D.D., Professional Speaker and Mentor,
Author of 41 published books,
Core Speaker for *Women of Faith* for 22 years

"Carole Brewer is one of the most genuine women of faith I've ever known. Her *Revitalize* study is a refreshing wash of truth and inspiration. Each page will challenge you to grow your faith and trust in God, even in the most difficult times. Thank you, Carole, for sharing your heart and journey with us — reminding us that while there are many good things we can do, the most important thing we do for ourselves and the ones we love is to refresh, renew, and revive our spirits every day."

— **Jennifer Strickland,** former model, speaker,
author of *Beautiful Lies, Girl Perfect,* and
More Beautiful Than You Know

"Honest, accessible and humorous, Carole Brewer's *Revitalize* delivers exactly what it promises: spiritual refreshment for all who navigate busy and demanding lives. Peppered with wonderfully personal insights and anecdotes, this devotional is also solidly grounded in the truths of Scripture and gently challenges with thought provoking questions. This is an appealing and uplifting book for one's personal journey or one shared with a group."

— **Marion MacKenzie Pyle,** M.A.,
Producer and Director for Legacy Media Lab,
Host, Speaker, Author of Healed, Healthy, *and Whole*

"What a fantastic new devotional on a needed topic by Carole Brewer. I couldn't put it down and highly recommend it to you! Bravo!

— **Marnie Swedberg,** Perspective Transformation Author,
Speaker & Radio Host,
Founder of *WomenSpeakers.com*

"This devotional is a download from heaven. Carole is a gifted writer but what is different about this devotional is God's signature is everywhere; without a doubt the Holy Spirit and Carole did this together."

— **Maralee Dawn,** President Maralee Dawn Ministries,
Director Daystar TV Canada,
Host of *Passionate Women* and *Maralee Dawn and Friends*

"Revitalize is the resource whose time has come! When I first read through the pages of this engaging devotional, I was immediately encouraged with grace, hope, and love. Inspirational and biblically-sound, Revitalize challenges me to genuinely examine my conscience and live beyond mediocrity into the fullness of God. It's wonderful to have a source that captures the true heart of transformation."

— **Kim Renga,** D.A., Communications and Educational Consultant,
Founder of *Reimagining Life Today!*

"Carole Brewer's expertly written devotional is a refuge for the soul and a bold reminder that peace is only found in God's presence. This book is a gift to the body of Christ."

— **Deborah Smith Pegues,** CPA/MBA, TV Host,
Author of *30 Days to Taming Your Tongue (one million sold)*
and *Emergency Prayers*

"I enjoyed Carole Brewer's devotional, "Revitalize - Refresh, Renew and Revive Your Spirit Now". It is full of wonderful testimonies, has a great outline for pondering the Word of God, and includes stories taken from her own life. I love that it is not just a daily devotional with a static devotion for the day, but presents questions and leaves room to prayerfully seek God for insight and understanding. I like how the book is organized with reoccurring daily themes for each week. My personal favorite is "A Spa for My Heart". We as women so desperately need spa days for our heart and spirit! Carole's book is a beautiful medley of scriptures, stories, songs, devotionals, and questions that make it a perfect book for a women's study or just your own personal devotional. Knowing Carole personally, I sense her heart and spirit in the pages of this sweet devotional that is sure to "Revitalize" those who read it. Thank you for sharing your heart and life with us Carole!"

— **Carol Doyel,** Author, Speaker,
Editor-in-Chief and Founder of *LivingBetter50.com*

Revitalize

Refresh, Renew & Revive
Your Spirit Now

CAROLE BREWER

A Six-Week Devotional
for Personal or Group Study

Published by
CAROLE BREWER
Ministries

Revitalize

Refresh, Renew & Revive Your Spirit *Now*

Copyright ©2018 by Carole Brewer *CaroleBrewer.com*

Published in the United States of America

Cover Design by Terri Podlenski, SmartCreativeLab.com

Layout Design by Surendra Gupta

Back cover photo by Susan Maxwell Skinner

Other photos and illustrations:
Carole Brewer ©2018
Microsoft Office Media Library ©2007
Shutterstock, Inc.©2003-2018

ISBN-13: 978-1724222251

ISBN-10: 1724222252

Christian Women – Religious Life – Worship and Devotion – Bible Study

Carole Brewer Ministries
P.O. Box 628 • Fair Oaks, California 95628

Dedication

To my Lord and Savior, Jesus Christ
for giving me the confidence to move forward;
all for His glory!

Contents

Week One : A New Beginning

Week Two : Another New Beginning

Week Three : Another New Beginning

Week Four : Another New Beginning

Week Five : Another New Beginning

Carole Brewer

Week Six : Another New Beginning

About the Author

Acknowledgments

Thank you to my husband Jan Brewer who brought me to the Lord, became my wonderful husband, and has encouraged me ever since to sing, speak, and write for God's glory!

With many thanks to Marnie Swedberg, Suellen Roberts, and Terri Podlenski whose ongoing support and wise counsel have been paramount to my ministry.

To my reading team: Kathy, Ruth, and Judy. Thank you for your time, insights, suggestions, encouragement, and prayers.

With special thanks to Bev Steerman and Kim Renga for their diligence to work with me over several long hours to enhance this book.

To our church couples group for keeping me in prayer as I worked on this project.

To my friends and associates for the kind reviews and support for my ministry, thank you.

With sincere gratitude to my ministry prayer team for faithfully praying over my prayer requests for 20+ years!

.

Greetings from Carole

Blessings and welcome to my devotional for women, an expression of God's love from my heart to yours.

We all have seasons in life when we need a spiritual lift. Life is a series of tests and a fresh breeze from the Holy Spirit is so needed during and after each trial. Many of us are emotionally hanging on the edge dealing with finances, family and health issues, loss and grief, unfulfilled expectations, and the constant disturbing news in our world.

I understand. God has revitalized me through many trials and in the process I've gained some spiritual resilience.

Please hear my heart for you, dear reader. Take time with each section to consider what you believe and determine how it lines up with God's Word. Then as you move forward to a closer relationship with Jesus, you'll find your spirit refreshed, your faith strengthened, and you'll have a heart overflowing with God's love.

May God richly bless and revitalize your journey.

In Christ always,

Week One

A New Beginning

Enlighten Up

DAY 1 - Paddle Forward

I've always loved rides that inspire me to sound off with a loud "Whee!" or "Yee-haw!" While visiting the Canadian Rockies, my husband and I decided to try a white-water raft trip.

After wriggling into wetsuits, rubber booties, and life jackets, we received a crash course in dry dock on rowing etiquette.

- *Paddle forward*
- *Paddle backward*
- *Stop*
- *Paddles up*
- *Rest*

Those commands seemed easy enough to follow.

Our group of seven gripped the side-ropes of our raft and lugged it downhill to the river's edge—a pebbly beach just around the bend from the bottom of the magnificent, roaring Athabasca Falls!

Quickly choosing our seats, we braced ourselves while our guide at the back calmly said, "Ready? Paddle forward." In less than a minute, we were bouncing through frothy swirls—the kind you'd find inside a giant Maytag operating in the heavy load cycle.

Paddling forward through the suds and working hard at it, we encountered *holes*, *pour-overs*, and other types of swirls found in a rushing river. I shouted to my crewmates as the icy water splashed against my cheeks, "I'm having a glacial facial!"

Five miles into our ten-mile trek, our guide gave us a surprising break. By following his commands, we maneuvered our rubber boat into an "eddy"—a calm pool of almost still water located on the backside of a huge protruding boulder. With rapids encircling us, it was amazing to rest and be protected from all the turbulence.

With his clear and specific commands, our guide made it possible for our team of paddlers to negotiate twenty sets of rapids and enjoy relaxing floats in-between.

And then with the white-water behind us, our guide again piped up, "Would anyone like to give my job a try?" Without a second thought, I jumped up thinking I would excel at the seemingly simple task. He handed me his larger paddle and I took his seat in the back of the raft.

"Ready? ...Mush!" I jokingly ordered.

As my group rowed, we immediately started turning to the left. Trying to conceal my embarrassment, I exclaimed in my best tour-guide voice, "We are now rotating. Just keep paddling and enjoy the view!" They all laughed and we completed our turn. Again I tried, saying, "Paddle forward!" The patient crew paddled with me into a second turn to the left and then a third. Exasperated with our dizzy course, I humbly and gratefully relinquished my seat of authority back to our expert guide.

What had I missed? Other than responding to our guide's voice commands coming from behind, the scenery and action ahead drew most of my attention. I didn't know how a rudder works; in this case his big paddle. A rudder, according to the dictionary, is a vertical blade at the stern of a vessel that can be turned horizontally to change the vessel's direction when in motion. Our guide did just that making our efforts to paddle forward a success.

Through this exhilarating and *refreshing* experience, I've learned that without the presence of our eternal Guide, we can take meaningless life-spirals. When relinquishing our will to God's, the life-journeys we take, complete with serene pools and torrent rapids, will go forward in His divine direction and bring glory to His name.

> "Trust God from the bottom of your heart; don't try to figure out everything on your own. Listen for God's voice in everything you do, everywhere you go; he's the one who will keep you on track," (Proverbs 3:5-6 MSG).

> "You make known to me the path of life; you will fill me with joy in your presence, with eternal pleasures at your right hand," (Psalm 16:11).

Just between God & me:

1. Do you remember any wasted turns in your life? What happened?

_____

_____

_____

_____

_____

_____

_____

_____

_____

_____

_____

_____

_____

_____

_____

_____

2. How and when has God demonstrated to you that He is the Solid Rock who gives shelter and peace in your life?

_____

_____

_____

_____

_____

_____

_____

_____

_____

_____

_____

_____

3. When trials have encircled you, how has God protected you from the turbulence?

_____

_____

_____

_____

_____

_____

_____

_____

_____

_____

_____

Thoughts for sharing with others:

_____
_____
_____
_____
_____
_____
_____
_____
_____
_____
_____
_____
_____
_____
_____
_____
_____
_____
_____
_____
_____
_____
_____
_____
_____
_____
_____
_____
_____
_____
_____

Renewing My Trust

DAY 2 - Name Them

Let's admit it. To renew our trust in God, we have to name the hurts and discouragements that have caused us to need our faith revitalized. A friend once told me, "you have to purge the puss before healing can begin." Ouch! Yes, it does hurt, but by identifying the source, we know what to relinquish into God's hands.

Personally, I've been disappointed many times for not getting certain things I thought I wanted. I've been snubbed and rejected over the years in different competitive situations. I've experienced grief over the loss of loved ones, and I'm not crazy about getting older. I could give you my entire list, but I think you get the picture.

Compared to most people, I'm just about normal. Life situations can get me down and away from where I need to be; in God's presence and in His Word.

Our enemy, Satan, is an angel but a fallen one with no interest in guarding us. He has targeted me with the intention of destroying my life, and you're not exempt from his plans either. (1 Peter 5:8) Satan is our #1 enemy who uses all the unhappy, frustrating, tragic but common life occurrences to dis-courage us. Extracting courage from you and me is what he excels in!

Satan's main weapons are lies and his purpose is to keep us away from God's Word. It's a spiritual battle we can't see, but oh, it's all around us! Just turn on the news.

"For our struggle is not against flesh and blood, but against the rulers, against the authorities, against the powers of this dark world and against the spiritual forces of evil in the heavenly realms," (Ephesians 6:12).

Our only defense against our enemy's schemes is God's Word, the sword of the Spirit! (Ephesians 6:17) It's very powerful, but it takes practice to use it well. When I was growing up, my great-grandparent's 1871 Bible was concealed under a pile of books and magazines. That beautiful sword was hidden from view and its cutting, dividing, double-edged capabilities were far away from my family's consciousness.

Let's name the hurts and discouragements…and the enemy who seeks to grow our emotional pain like cancer. Then, we can uncover the truth, root out the debilitating hurts, and open both our hearts and minds to learn, practice, and trust God's Word again! He is our Healer.

"I will tell you what is written in the Book of Truth," (Daniel 10:21).

"All Scripture is God-breathed and is useful for teaching, rebuking, correcting and training in righteousness, 17 so that the servant of God may be thoroughly equipped for every good work," (2 Timothy 3:16-17).

"I have told you these things, so that in me you may have peace. In this world, you will have trouble. But take heart! I have overcome the world" (John 16:33).

Just between God & me:

1. What recent hurts can you name?

_____

_____

_____

_____

_____

_____

_____

_____

2. Can you name the things that are keeping you from completely trusting God?

_____

_____

_____

_____

_____

_____

_____

_____

3. What discouragers does Satan most often use to taunt you?

_____

_____

_____

_____

_____

_____

_____

_____

4. Starting a conversation with God is the best way to re-establish your relationship. What do you want to tell Him? He's ready and listening.

_____

_____

_____

_____

_____

_____

_____

Thoughts for sharing with others:

_____

_____

_____

_____

_____

_____

_____

_____

_____

_____

_____

_____

_____

_____

_____

_____

_____

_____

Getting the Tangles Out

DAY 3 - The Octopus Lifestyle

I arrived at this description one day while sitting on my living room rug surrounded by stacks of papers. It was overwhelming to be encircled by piles of bills, medical records, letters, etc, and more etceteras. With only two arms, I could have used eight!

Here's a quick quiz:

- ○ *I'm ready to throw in the...*
- ○ *I'm just a bundle of...*
- ○ *I can't take it...*
- ○ *My life is falling...*

All of your answers are correct! Here's the last one:

○ *I feel like resigning from the human...*

Race. Is that about who we are or does it mean running around in circles? For me, it's both.

What multiple roles in life we play! We could be known as a daughter, sister, wife, mom, grandma, girlfriend, or neighbor. Being responsible for ourselves and others would be enough but life piles on a lot more! Many of us help with our extended families too. And then there is housework—cooking, cleaning, laundry, repairs, pet care... can you think of more? Employment outside of the home is a huge one! Volunteering may be on your agenda along with prayer and devotion time. What about social networking and exercise? There is an endless list of to-do's and want-to-do's. I'm thanking the Lord that you're reading this since it means you've made time for God too!

The writer of Hebrews puts it this way:

*"Therefore, since we have so great a cloud of witnesses surrounding us, let us throw off everything that hinders and the sin that so easily **entangles**. And let us run with perseverance the race marked out for us, fixing our eyes on Jesus, the pioneer, and perfecter of faith,"* (Hebrews12:1-2).

As we deal with an Octopus Lifestyle, we're going to have to trust God to show us how to order our steps and organize our days, all for His glory.

"Cast all your anxiety on him because he cares for you," (1 Peter 5:7).

Just between God & me:

1. With all of your responsibilities, how often do you find yourself feeling overwhelmed and in tangles?

_____

_____

_____

_____

_____

_____

_____

_____

2. How do you normally deal with stress?

_____

_____

_____

_____

_____

_____

_____

3. What legs of your octopus (responsibilities) could you down-size or even cut off to make your days more manageable?

_____

_____

_____

_____

_____

_____

_____

4. How do you plan to take time for resting in His presence this week?

_____

_____

_____

_____

_____

_____

_____

_____

Thoughts for sharing with others:

_____

_____

_____

_____

_____

_____

_____

_____

_____

_____

_____

_____

_____

_____

_____

_____

_____

_____

_____

Rediscovering Me

DAY 4 - Now I See

I was born cross-eyed and legally blind in my left eye. At age nine, a wonderful eye surgeon moved my lazy eye to the center greatly improving my outward appearance. I've been blessed throughout my life to have fairly good vision due to my healthy, strong eye on the right.

My greater disability was my ignorance of God's love and sacrifice for me. While growing up, the only understanding I had of the Bible was through movies or TV evangelists.

In college my friends faithfully shared their belief in Jesus, but my spiritual blind spots and out-of-focus thinking kept me from comprehending their words. I was certain a heavenly point system existed, and any points I lost were irretrievable. Feeling guilt and shame, I reasoned that religion would just go away if I stopped thinking about it.

The Gideons came on campus and handed out bright green New Testaments to whoever would take one. I reluctantly accepted my copy from a music major friend. Worried that someone would notice, I quickly hid that glowing, oscillating little book in my purse.

In a secluded spot on campus, I opened the New Testament and scanned the index. Topic titles like Afraid, Anxious, Discouraged, and Needing Rules for Living first caught my attention. Continuing to flip through the pages, I stopped at the inside back cover. After a long stare, I signed my name under the title "My Decision to Receive Christ as My Savior". Since my plans were falling apart, I thought I'd give God a try.

16

Just two weeks later, my husband to be, Jan Brewer, invited me to a Christian rally at the California Exposition race track. What a spiritual place that was! I wore a straw hat and sunglasses just planning to check out the event plus enjoy an evening with Jan.

Leighton Ford gave a stirring message and asked those who would like to make a decision for Christ to stand. Fully intending to stay seated, I stood up! Then, I stepped out, walked down several flights of stairs, and found myself on the grassy area in front of the speaker's platform. All my harbored trials and frustrations seemed to slide out of my toes and I felt a warmth and presence I'd never felt before. That evening, I received the indwelling of the Holy Spirit and became a child of the King!

My spiritual blind spots and out-of-focus thinking have changed. Now I see! Overwhelmed by God's love for me, I found my new life in Jesus Christ. When I see Him face to face in heaven, it will be with 20/20 vision.

"Taste and see that the Lord is good; blessed is the one who takes refuge in him," (Psalm 34:8).

"Blessed are the pure in heart, for they will see God," (Matthew 5:8).

Just between God & me:

Before receiving two corrective surgeries, I experienced name-calling for most of my elementary school years.

1. Have you ever been bullied or made fun of because of your outward appearance?

    _____

    _____

    _____

    _____

    _____

    _____

2. Have you ever made fun of someone else's appearance? Do you remember how that made you feel at the time? If so, how do you feel about it now?

    _____

    _____

    _____

    _____

    _____

    _____

    _____

3. As you receive God's forgiveness, in what ways can you show His forgiveness to others?

    _____

    _____

    _____

    _____

    _____

    _____

4. How has God demonstrated His love for you in a specific situation?

_____

_____

_____

_____

_____

_____

_____

_____

Thoughts for sharing with others:

_____

_____

_____

_____

_____

_____

_____

_____

_____

_____

_____

_____

_____

_____

_____

_____

_____

_____

Day 5 - Surrender Pray Arise

A SPA *for My Heart*

How do you feel about letting someone hands-on pamper, fix, or enhance you? Do you love it or not? Or maybe you've never been to a spa thinking it's frivolous, too indulgent, or costly.

I'm not exactly sure of Peter's reasoning, but he said to Jesus, *"Master, you wash my feet?"* Jesus answered, *"You don't understand now what I'm doing, but it will be clear enough to you later."* Peter persisted, *"You're not going to wash my feet—ever!"*

Pride or false humility could have been why Peter turned down our Savior's offer to serve him.

Jesus said, "If I don't wash you, you can't be part of what I'm doing."

"Master!" said Peter. "Not only my feet, then. Wash my hands! Wash my head!" (John 13:6-9 MSG).

SURRENDER

✟ In all situations, I can depend on Jesus to direct my course

My thoughts _____

_____

✟ If I name my hurts and discouragements, then I can give them to Jesus.

My thoughts _____

_____

✝ When I organize my days, I can bring glory to God.

My thoughts _____

_____

✝ Enough of my out-of-focus thinking. I need God's truth.

My thoughts _____

_____

"Repent, then, and turn to God, so that your sins may be wiped out, that times of refreshing may come from the Lord," (Acts 3:19).

PRAY

Taking time to converse with my Father God through Jesus Christ, His Son, and through His Holy Spirit:

ADORATION : expressing my love
Proclaiming God's magnificence by speaking His attributes and singing His praises. (i.e. His greatness, goodness, glory, love)

CONFESSION : admitting my sin
My thoughts and deeds that have dishonored God:

PRAYER PROMPT

Forgive me Father when I don't take time to meditate on Your word and apply it to my life.

SUPPLICATION: asking God to help me
(i.e., health, responsibilities, time-stretching, peace, restored joy)

INTERCESSION: asking God to help others
(i.e., health, responsibilities, time-stretching, peace, restored joy)
Standing in the gap for those who don't know God.

THANKSGIVING: expressing deepest gratitude
Speaking and singing from your heart.

ARISE

"I instruct you in the way of wisdom and lead you along straight paths. When you walk, your steps will not be hampered; when you run, you will not stumble" (Proverbs 4:11-12).

"Ask and it will be given to you; seek and you will find; knock and the door will be opened to you," (Matthew 7:7).

"I am the light of the world. Whoever follows me will never walk in darkness, but will have the light of life," (John 8:12).

A Song to Bless

I'm Walkin' With My Lord Today
Words & music by Carole Brewer

I was walkin' down that lonely road
before I knew my Lord
But now Jesus is keepin' me company
and we're walkin' in one accord
Before I sought His holy presence,
my path was as dark as night
But now He's a lamp unto my feet,
my bright and shining light, …whoa…

I'm walkin' with my Lord today
I can feel His mighty power every time I pray
Well, I've asked Him in my heart and He's come to stay
And I'm walkin' with my Lord today

I was unaware that Jesus was there
before I asked Him into my heart
It used to be that it was just me and myself,
But now my Lord and I are never apart
Wherever we go, whatever we do,
He is always by my side
And all that I am I owe to Him,
let His name be glorified, whoa,

I'm walkin' with my Lord today
I can feel His mighty power every time I pray
Well, I've asked Him in my heart and He's come to stay
And I'm walkin' with my Lord today

Week Two

Another New Beginning

Enlighten Up

Day 1 - The Smashing Photo Shoot

As a singer-speaker-recording artist, I've had my picture taken many times over the years. Some of my friends have told me I'm photogenic. Hmm. Well, I'm not camera shy and I've found the hard work of preparing for a professional photo session to be enjoyable.

There is one exception, though, it'my appointment for a mammogram. Yikes! Can you relate? It's the smashing but necessary, depth-perceiving photo shoot requiring no makeup, hair styling, or wardrobe consideration other than you go topless!

Discomfort is the real issue, right? The rest of the prep and waiting goes pretty quickly since getting in and out of the lab takes about 45 minutes. Why then does this type of event stand out in my memory above root canals?

During one of my past appointments, the technician gently lifted and positioned the front left side of my upper torso onto the scanner. Then, she compressed that portion between the upper and lower flat-bed screens. Very uncomfortable but so far, nothing was unusual.

"Hold your breath," she said as she went behind a screen to start the scan. I took a deep breath and held it. The machine began humming as the scanning beds squeezed me in and then BLACKOUT! All power in the room ceased, and I was in that machine. The room became very quiet, the technician became very quiet, and those depressing moments seemed much longer.

Suddenly, the auxiliary power came on and that scanner popped open. Ah, sweet release!

So what spiritual application can be applied from this type of experience? Well, it could be about attitude. It wasn't the tech's fault the power failed and there was a backup plan in place. Did I get mad? Inwardly scared, I guess. But then, the machine did pop open to my relief! With the power back on and after having a good laugh, the technician and I finished up.

One week later the good news came that no cancer was detected. Praise God again!

"A cheerful heart is good medicine, but a crushed spirit dries up the bones," (Proverbs 17:22).

Listening to the Holy Spirit
and following His lead
greatly affects how we see life
and how others see us.

Just between God & me:

1. What recent opportunities have you had to demonstrate to others and to yourself, peace, cheerfulness, and mercy?

Peace _____

_____

Cheerfulness _____

_____

Mercy _____

_____

Thoughts for sharing with my group:

_____
_____
_____
_____
_____
_____
_____
_____
_____
_____
_____
_____
_____
_____
_____
_____
_____
_____
_____
_____
_____
_____
_____
_____
_____
_____
_____
_____
_____
_____
_____
_____

Renewing My Trust

Day 2 - Consider

In today's vast global connections, the number of messages and narratives we're exposed to are staggering. Our minds are intensely targeted as the world vies for our attention, attacks our beliefs, and attempts to rob us of our finances.

First, consider that there are hundreds of groups ascribing to an established religion founded by a strong leader. Some are many centuries old, and some are relatively newer being in existence for less than 200 years. Even Atheism qualifies as a religion since not believing in a god is also a belief system.

Those closest to us: family members, neighbors, co-workers, teachers, financial advisors, and doctors all have opportunities to express their views and influence how we think about life in general and our purpose here on earth.

But because of advanced technology, probably the most powerful earthly force that influences us today is media: television, videos, radio, podcasts, movies, and all social networking. So many forms of media are attention grabbing and can sink messages deep into our psyche if we don't have a strong belief system in place.

More great thought-changers are books, magazines, live theater, and concerts. In cities there are all types of outdoor signage and giant screens like the ones in Times Square.

Quite simply, unless we're out of cell tower range, media bombards us daily.

Consider what the Apostle Paul wrote in 2 Timothy 4:3-5,

> *"For the time will come when people will not put up with sound doctrine. Instead, to suit their own desires, they will gather around them a great number of teachers to say what their itching ears want to hear. They will turn their ears away from the truth and turn aside to myths. But you, keep your head in all situations."*

Paul also wrote in Ephesians 4:14,

> *"...we will no longer be infants, tossed back and forth by the waves, and blown here and there by every wind of teaching and by the cunning and craftiness of people in their deceitful scheming."*

Then, in Philippians 4:8, Paul says to us,

> *"Finally, brothers and sisters, whatever is true, whatever is noble, whatever is right, whatever is pure, whatever is lovely, whatever is admirable—if anything is excellent or praiseworthy—think about such things."*

The truths found throughout God's
Word are relevant to us today.
Within the 66 books of the Bible,
there are no contradictions.

Just between God & me:

Based on the above Bible passages:

1. What do you think Paul is saying to you with his statement? *"But you, keep your head in all situations."*

_____

_____

_____

_____

_____

_____

_____

_____

_____

2. What kinds of distractions cause you to drift away from your relationship with Jesus?

_____

_____

_____

_____

_____

_____

_____

_____

3. What type of *spiritual* boat are you in right now? Are you anchored or drifting?

_____

_____

_____

_____

_____

_____

_____

_____

4. What choices can you make about the types of media messages you listen to?

_____

_____

_____

_____

_____

_____

_____

_____

Thoughts for sharing with my group:

_____

_____

_____

_____

_____

_____

_____

_____

_____

_____

_____

_____

_____

_____

_____

_____

_____

_____

_____

_____

_____

_____

_____

_____

_____

_____

_____

_____

_____

_____

_____

_____

_____

Getting the Tangles Out

DAY 3 - Growth on Hold

Have you ever seen pictures of The Butchart Gardens? It's over 100 years old, is located on Vancouver Island in British Colombia, and is one of Canada's historical treasures.

When my husband and I visited there, our eyes beheld one of the most beautiful gardens in the world. It was especially breathtaking to behold the centerpiece of the estate; the gorgeous Sunken Garden. "This is what heaven must look like," my husband remarked. And when I thought even more about the garden's heavenly appearance, I thought it could also be a picture of our lives.

You may be thinking, "That's a very nice thought Carole, but let's get REAL! That garden sounds like a unique, tranquil, well-groomed repose. My life is anything but that; more like a weed patch! I'm just hanging on, trying to survive every day, and it's hard to see any flowers blooming in my life right now." Okay, I hear you so let me further explain.

Before the Sunken Garden was a beautiful oasis of color with thriving plants, flowers, and trees, it was a parched, barren rock quarry. Perhaps that's how you picture your life now; being exhausted and parched from long-suffering.

Mrs. Butchart's solution for change over a century ago, was to order a huge shipment of rich topsoil for that barren place. Then, the soil was cultivated; broken down into fine soft pieces so it could receive and nourish new plant roots. With plenty of sunshine and water, the environment was perfect for growth. (Mark 4:3-9)

Life is hard, but the trials we face are like cultivators for the heart; a way God can break down our pride and hurts into fine soft pieces of humility and surrender. On our journey, many faith entanglers will continue to intersect our path putting our spiritual growth on hold. With God's help, our cultivated hearts will overcome, grow stronger, and be pliable to let the truth of His Word take even better root than before. All the victory will be His, and our life will be more beautiful to behold.

"So then, just as you received Christ Jesus as Lord, continue to live your lives in him, rooted and built up in him," *(Colossians 2:6-7).*

THE HOLY SPIRIT BLOOMS THROUGH US AND FORTIFIES US WITH...

Soil/Nutrients:
from God's word
2 Timothy 3:16-17

"Living Water" and "Light" from the Son John 4:10, 8:12

"Oxygen" The presence of the Holy Spirit Job 33:4

JESUS BREATHED ON THEM AND SAID, "RECEIVE THE HOLY SPIRIT." JOHN 20:22

Carole Brewer

Just between God & me:

1. Name the distractions that keep the truth of God's Word from taking root in your heart?

_____

_____

_____

_____

_____

_____

_____

2. Does your heart feel hardened; determined to stay angry and hold a grudge? How can you allow the Holy Spirit to cultivate and prepare your heart for a new season of growth?

_____

_____

_____

_____

_____

_____

3. Do you ever feel exhausted and parched from long-suffering? What gardening tips from the Holy Spirit will help you recover, grow, and thrive?

_____

_____

_____

_____

_____

_____

4. What plans can you make to take time for rest, renewal, and to breathe in God's presence this week?

_____

_____

_____

_____

_____

_____

Thoughts for sharing with my group:

_____

_____

_____

_____

_____

_____

_____

_____

_____

_____

_____

_____

_____

_____

_____

_____

_____

_____

_____

Rediscovering Me

Day 4 - Short

My height is 5'2" so please note that "vertically challenged" is the politically correct term for my stature.

When shopping for clothes, I head straight for the stores that stock garments designed for women who are tiny, trim, short, and squatty. It's the Petite Department! For me, it's a triumph whenever I find something at a good price that fits. Honestly, since choices are limited, searching for outfits proportioned for vertically challenged women can be a tough assignment. If you're height is average, count your blessings. Your Misses' department usually has a huge inventory in comparison.

Once in awhile, if there's a great sale going on, I'll try on a Misses size top...just in case. Looking in the mirror, I take hold of the shoulder seams and pull them up to my ears. Voila! Looks great! Oh well.

But when it comes to being short,

"There is no difference, for all have sinned and fall SHORT of the glory of God." (Romans 3:22-23).

Luke records in Chapter 19:1-10 that short Zacchaeus, a wealthy tax collector, climbed up a tree so he could spot Jesus walking amongst the crowd. *"When Jesus reached the spot, he looked up and said to him, "Zacchaeus, come down immediately. I must stay at your house today."* Wow! What would people think? Jesus was socializing with a sinner! Short Zacchaeus, overwhelmed that Jesus would honor him, responded with a changed heart saying, *"Look, Lord! Here and now I give half of my possessions to the poor, and if I have cheated anybody out of anything, I will pay back four times the amount." Jesus said to him,"Today salvation has come to this house...For the Son of Man came to seek and to save what was lost."*

In the spiritual sense, we are all vertically challenged; we all need a Savior.

> *"There is no difference"*, whether short, medium, or tall, *"...all have sinned and fall **short** of the glory of God, and all are justified freely by his grace through the redemption that came by Christ Jesus,"* (Romans 3:22-24).

So when you think SHORT, think:

> *"The name of the Lord is a strong tower; the righteous run to it and are safe"*, (Proverbs 18:10 NKJV).

Carole Brewer

Just between God & me:

1. In what ways can you depend on our Lord to help you where you fall short?

_____

_____

_____

_____

_____

_____

_____

2. Are you willing to surrender your past to God so He can turn it around for His glory? If so, what changes will you make to reflect your decision?

_____

_____

_____

_____

_____

_____

_____

3. Which songs of worship help you overcome fear and discouragement?

_____

_____

_____

_____

_____

_____

_____

Thoughts for sharing with my group:

_____

_____

_____

_____

_____

_____

_____

_____

_____

_____

_____

_____

_____

_____

_____

_____

_____

_____

_____

_____

_____

_____

_____

_____

_____

_____

_____

_____

_____

_____

_____

Day 5 - Surrender Pray Arise

SURRENDER

✟ Being in tune with the Holy Spirit affects how I look at life and how others view me.

My thoughts _____

_____

✟ Since what I see and hear can influence me, I need to remind myself daily of Philippines 4:8.

My thoughts _____

_____

✝ I will identify the entanglers that put my spiritual growth on hold.

My thoughts _____

_____

✝ I sincerely confess the areas of my life where I fall short and trust God for a new start in Him.

My thoughts _____

_____

PRAY

Let us then approach God's throne of grace
with confidence,
so that we may receive mercy and find grace to
help us in our time of need. Hebrews 4:16

ADORATION : expressing my love
Proclaiming God's magnificence by speaking His attributes and singing His praises (i.e. His greatness, goodness, glory, love)

CONFESSION : admitting my sin
My thoughts and deeds that have dishonored God:

PRAYER PROMPT

*I confess that I am best and
strongest in Your presence.*

SUPPLICATION: asking God to help me
(i.e., health, responsibilities, time-stretching, peace, restored joy)

INTERCESSION: asking God to help others
(i.e., health, responsibilities, time-stretching, peace, restored joy)
Standing in the gap for those who don't know God

THANKSGIVING: expressing deepest gratitude
Speaking and singing from your heart.

ARISE

*"See, I am doing a new thing! Now it springs up; do you
not perceive it? I am making a way in the wilderness and
streams in the wasteland,"*(Isaiah 43:19).

"Do not grieve, for the joy of the Lord is your strength,"
(Nehemiah 8:10).

*"Wake up, sleeper, rise from the dead,and Christ will shine
on you."* (Ephesians 5:14).

A Song to Bless

Return to Your First Love

Words & Music by Carole Brewer

Return to your first love, return to your first love
Remember when your heart was young?
Return to your first love
Jesus your first love
Remember all that He has done?
Remember God's only Son.

Return to your first love, remember your first love
Return your life to Him
Return to your first love
Jesus your first love
Remember what your heart said then?
Give Him your heart again.

What time or season did your thoughts stray
From the One who calls you His own?
What was the reason your heart turned away
from your Lord, your God alone?
The Lord's still gracious, abounding in love,
And His promises are forever true
Return your heart to Almighty God
And He will return to you.

Return to your first love, remember your first love
Return your life to Him
Return to your first love
Jesus, your first love
Remember what your heart said then?
Give Him your heart again

Week Three

Another New Beginning

Enlighten Up

DAY 1 - Sing for Joy ... Anyway

If you've ever sung on a live TV show, you'll agree there's nothing like it! When the red light on the camera comes on, you're it! A cold, drafty studio combined with jittery nerves already sets up the singer for a less-than-perfect, teeth-chattering solo. Even the most carefully placed stance on the assigned spot cannot overt the bloopers waiting to happen.

With cameras rolling, I've had earrings drop off, moths upstage me in front of the lens, and a set backdrop crash to the floor. During one of my tender ballads, viewers were distracted by my fluorescent red tongue—the result of finishing a cherry cough drop just before the camera came on.

There's nothing like singing for a live audience either; faces are looking right back at you and reacting ...or maybe not.

I sang for a women's luncheon at a church located next to a fire station. Imagine getting to sing with an accompaniment track mixed with incoming distress calls. At another event, the emcee moved up my introduction by ten minutes. I heard her read my bio followed by welcoming applause while seated in the ladies room.

Such mentionable mishaps can only be rivaled by my close encounters with a variety of critters.

During a Sunday morning service, a squirrel ran straight across the sanctuary carpet to the front pew where I was seated. Lifting my feet straight out, I voiced a high "Whee" as the petrified rodent darted directly under my seat. Somehow, the dignified introduction I'd just received from the pastor lost its credibility.

Aviating bugs lodged in my teeth at a Fourth of July concert in the park. At a formal concert, a fly darted in as my jaw dropped for the magnificent high note. It buzzed around and zoomed out. Was that a critique?

Cows, on the other hand, love my singing! At a small country church surrounded by a large field, the local herd gathered just outside the open windows. Contented and seeming to sway to my music, they were udderly mooooved!

Putting yourself out there does have its risks, but I've learned that attention-grabbing mishaps can turn into great blessings and cause me to sing for joy—anyway!

"Our mouths were filled with laughter, our tongues with songs of joy. Then it was said among the nations, "The Lord has done great things for them." (Psalm 126:2)

Just between God & me:

1. What kinds of mishaps have you had that you can laugh about afterward?

_____

_____

_____

_____

_____

_____

_____

_____

_____

2. In what situations have you been able to sing for joy... anyway?

_____

_____

_____

_____

_____

_____

_____

_____

Thoughts I can share with my group:

_____

_____

_____

_____

_____

_____

_____

_____

_____

_____

_____

_____

_____

_____

_____

_____

_____

Renewing My Trust

DAY 2 - Discern

Can you always tell the difference between truth and a lie?

We mortals can have a hard time discerning just as Eve did in the garden. (Genesis 3:1-4) The enemy, disguised as a nice-guy, slithered up to her and asked, *"Did God really say?"* With doubt planted in her mind, the woman started reasoning through God's rules for fruit selection. The serpent nailed down his lie by saying, *"You surely will not die."* Famous last words!

Any messages delivered by Satan are intended to rush and push us into doing something. He's the master discourager and is relentless in creating confusion, causing obsessive worry, and propagating fear. He condemns us and pours on large doses of guilt and shame. Don't be fooled by his pleasant appearance; when Satan speaks it is for the destruction of our souls. (2 Cor. 11:14)

In contrast to the serpent in the garden, Jesus walked 42 miles to meet with a Samaritan woman and address her great pain. (John 4:16-18) Jesus knew her five husbands had divorced her and she was living with another man. In that culture, a husband could legally divorce his wife for many reasons including not producing sons or putting too much salt in his food. Jesus understood the woman's many failed relationships and replied in a kind voice, *"What you have said is quite true."* By affirming her honesty, giving her the gift of time, and talking with her when Jews don't ever speak to Samaritans, we now have a record and proof of Jesus' high regard for women. During their conversation, the woman said, *"I know that Messiah is coming."* Then Jesus declared, *"I, the one speaking to you—I am he."*

When God speaks to us, it's most often in a gentle whisper. His Holy Spirit leads and confirms our actions as we pray and learn His Word. God's voice is reassuring, encouraging, calming, comforting, and convicting.

The Apostle Paul wrote in his letter to the church in Laodicea,

"...so that they may have the full riches of complete understanding, in order that they may know the mystery of God, namely, Christ, in whom are hidden all the treasures of wisdom and knowledge. I tell you this so that no one may deceive you by fine-sounding arguments," (Colossians 2:2-4). Paul also wrote another reassuring truth, *"Therefore, there is now no condemnation for those who are in Christ Jesus,"* (Romans 8:1).

Of all the leaders and founders of the many different world religions, only Jesus Christ has conquered death and the grave!

He is Alive!

Just between God & me:

1. Has anyone ever tried to convince you to make a quick decision without giving you a chance to think about it?

_____
_____
_____
_____
_____
_____
_____

2. In the past, what negative statements were spoken to you that caused you to be greatly discouraged?

_____
_____
_____
_____
_____
_____
_____

3. According to today's devotional, what or who is the ultimate source of your discouragement?

_____
_____
_____
_____
_____
_____
_____
_____

4. Hearing God's gentle whisper requires being still and quiet to listen. If you take time to listen right now, what is He saying to you?

_____

_____

_____

_____

_____

_____

_____

Thoughts I can share with my group:

_____

_____

_____

_____

_____

_____

_____

_____

_____

_____

_____

_____

_____

_____

_____

_____

_____

_____

Getting the Tangles Out

Day 3 - Leaking Zeal

One of God's greatest plans for us is that He allows us to leak! Yes, like a sieve! Think about it. If all His blessings were bestowed upon us when we first decided Jesus would be Lord of our lives, we could say, "That's it; I have it all. See you in heaven, God." Since we leak so profusely, our passion for serving dehydrates when we neglect to spend time with Jesus, the Living Water. Our God provides the need for us to return to Him daily for refilling.

Romans12 is one of my favorite guidelines for living. In verses 11-13, Paul exhorts us to, *"Never be lacking in zeal, but keep your spiritual fervor, serving the Lord. Be joyful in hope, patient in affliction, faithful in prayer. Share with the Lord's people who are in need. Practice hospitality."*

To do so takes passion!

Perhaps my acronym for **PASSION** will help us re-think the importance of daily relying on God's presence.

60

Persistence to follow - determined to walk forward in faith

Attitude adjustments - figuring out why I've lacked motivation

Sipping from His cup - renewing my covenant to holiness

Singing His praises - having the heart to rejoice in all situations

Infused with His Spirit - being given new strength to serve

One Vine - when connected to Jesus we bear much fruit

Never-ending love - sharing with deepest intimacy an eternal
relationship with our Lord and Savior

Jesus said, *"I am the vine and you are the branches. If you remain in me and I in you, you will bear much fruit. Apart from me you can do nothing,"* (John 15:5).

The Giver of Life re-fills our leaks. He wants to continually engage with us in an ongoing, active, equipping, and Spirit-led relationship. God is calling us to revitalize our passion for Him!

"To the thirsty I will give water without cost from the spring of the water of life." (Revelation 21:6).

Just between God & me:

1. If your desire to actively serve God has lessened, why do you think you feel that way?

_____

_____

_____

_____

_____

_____

_____

2. Are you disappointed in God for not granting you a prayer request you specifically asked of Him? If so, how has that made a difference in the way you view your relationship with God?

_____

_____

_____

_____

_____

_____

_____

3. What steps can you take today to revitalize your relationship with the Father, Son, and Holy Spirit?

_____

_____

_____

_____

_____

_____

Thoughts I can share with my group:

_____

_____

_____

_____

_____

_____

_____

_____

_____

_____

_____

_____

_____

_____

_____

_____

_____

_____

_____

_____

_____

_____

_____

_____

_____

_____

_____

_____

_____

_____

_____

Rediscovering Me

Day 4 - Measurements

When I aspired to become a singer, my ongoing pitfall was that I compared myself to others. Seeing performers on TV or repeatedly hearing songs on the radio by well-known artists, I thought I would never be good enough to succeed. Talk about defeat from the get-go. Of course, the enemy knew ahead of time my potential to become a Christian and write songs for God's glory. My opposition was so great in college, I almost quit singing completely.

The enemy, evil to the core, consistently sends subliminal negative messages to us through all kinds of media sources. Sadly, he may also use people who are close to us. In so many ways, he tells us that unless we measure up to the world's standards, we fail. How tragic that Satan's lies cause so much stress, resentment, depression, false pride, and addictions. Being a perfectionist but never satisfied was one of my traits.

But I became a Christian. Say Hallelujah with me!!! And then, I started the life-transforming process of infusing God's Word into my heart and mind. I found Galatians 6:4 to be the sledge hammer breaking my chains of low-self esteem. Take this truth in for yourself. *"Each one should test their own actions. Then they can take pride in themselves alone, without comparing themselves to someone else,"* (Galatians 6:4). That verse released me to sing. No longer looking to the right or left, I now look up for my approval.

God spoke through the prophet Jeremiah for his time and for us today.

"You will seek me and find me when you seek me with all your heart. I will be found by you," declares the LORD, "and will bring you back from captivity," (Jeremiah 29: 13-14).

Long before we were born, Jesus carried all of our guilt and faults with Him to the cross and left them there. Our self-worth is measured by His sacrifice for us. We are justified and completely forgiven because Jesus took our sin and gave us His righteousness. (Romans 5:15) Through Him, we have freedom and peace.

Just between God & me:

1. Have you ever quit something you loved because you felt you could never measure up to the success of others doing something similar? What about now?

   _____

   _____

   _____

   _____

   _____

   _____

   _____

   _____

   _____

   _____

   _____

   _____

   _____

2. In what ways are you allowing your circumstances to define your identity?

_____

_____

_____

_____

_____

_____

_____

3. Does your self-view depend on the opinions, rewards, and praises of others?

_____

_____

_____

_____

_____

_____

_____

4. How does knowing what God's declares about you make a difference in your sense of security and confidence?

_____

_____

_____

_____

_____

_____

_____

Thoughts I can share with my group:

_____
_____
_____
_____
_____
_____
_____
_____
_____
_____
_____
_____
_____
_____
_____
_____
_____
_____
_____
_____
_____
_____
_____
_____
_____
_____
_____
_____

Day 5 - Surrender Pray Arise

SURRENDER

✝ I trust God to give me supernatural joy to sing His praises, whatever the circumstance.

My thoughts _____

_____

✝ I will take time to listen for God's still small voice and trust the Holy Spirit to guide me in all wisdom and knowledge.

My thoughts _____

_____

✝ I surrender any loss of motivation and ask God to reignite my passion for serving Him again.

My thoughts _____

_____

✝ I confess that I am a unique creation in God's Kingdom, highly valued, and loved beyond measure.

My thoughts _____

_____

PRAY

"Then you will call upon me and come and pray to me, and I will listen to you," (Jeremiah 29:12).

ADORATION : expressing my love
Proclaiming God's magnificence by speaking His attributes and singing His praises. (i.e. His greatness, goodness, glory, love)

CONFESSION : admitting my sin
My thoughts and deeds that have dishonored God:

PRAYER PROMPT

I confess that when I've had a disappointment, I retreat from my schedule of prayer, study, and church.

SUPPLICATION: asking God to help me
(i.e., health, responsibilities, time-stretching, peace, restored joy)

INTERCESSION: asking God to help others
(i.e., health, responsibilities, time-stretching, peace, restored joy)
Standing in the gap for those who don't know God

THANKSGIVING: expressing deepest gratitude
Speaking and singing from your heart.

> *"That my soul may sing praise to Thee, and not be silent.
> O Lord my God, I will give thanks to Thee forever,"*
> **(Psalm 30:12, NASB).**

ARISE

> *"Arise, shine, for your light has come, and the glory of the Lord
> rises upon you,"* (Isaiah 60:1).

A Song to Bless

Morning Star

Words & Music by Carole Brewer
(2 Peter 1:19, Revelation 22:16)

In the night there was glittering light
Throughout a radiant sky
And as I saw, I searched in awe
for a star on which to rely
By the dawn, all my confusion
Had slowly faded from view
Then I looked, and then I saw You
I saw You

Morning Star, bright Morning Star
In my heart I know who You are
You came down from heaven afar
shining light for all the world to see
Morning Star shine through me

His angel came to proclaim,
He's the Son of the Most High.
He's the Light in the darkest night.
He's the star on which to rely.
And so, we have the promise
And I know, a new day will start
When the Morning Star arises
in your heart, in your heart

Morning Star, bright Morning Star
In my heart I know who You are
You came down from heaven afar
shining light for all the world to see
Morning Star shine through me

Carole Brewer

Week Four

Another New Beginning

Enlighten Up

DAY 1 – Drum Roll

One of the most rewarding times in my life was when my husband Jan, a professional drummer, and I had the opportunity to team-teach a music class for developmentally disabled adults. The Sacramento Association for Retarded Citizens approved our proposal to start a performing group and they helped us begin. The association's Activity Director then recruited for us the loudest and hammiest singers at summer camp.

After leading our class for several weeks without a specific goal, we amended our proposal to state, "We will continue as the teachers for this music class with the understanding that the participants will prepare a program and enter an upcoming performing arts competition."

Our students said, "Okay!" not realizing the challenging six months of hard work ahead of them. Gratefully, their parents agreed to continue their support.

During that hot Sacramento summer, in an available classroom with no air conditioning and a pathetic piano, we all pressed forward— putting together a half-hour program of pop, gospel, and patriotic songs. Besides musical training, we gave our seven adult students lessons in stage presence, social graces, and grooming. "Smile!" and "Let's try again!" came out of my mouth hundreds of times. I labeled our teaching style "creative repetition."

The anticipated October day arrived and it was our group's turn to perform before the audience and judges. Those long hours of rehearsal paid off because our songs went like clockwork. Amazed by the quality of our presentation, the audience gave us a huge round of applause after each musical selection. Trying to gather our composure with all of the excitement, we began our last song. Our drummer accidentally hit his knee on the bottom of the snare drum causing it to fly off its stand and roll down the center aisle through the audience. Dutifully, the rest of us followed our motto: "Keep going no matter what!" while Joe got up from his stool to chase the runaway drum. Catching it right in front of the judges, he quickly carried it back, re-positioned it on its stand, sat down, and grabbed a stick just in time to hit the last beat of the song. We won!

It was the beginning of seven of the most incredible years of our lives. The River City Good Time Band, born that day, grew into a model program for people with disabilities that would forever raise the standard of expectations for the mentally challenged.

"Commit your way to the Lord; trust in him and he will do this," *(Psalm 37:5).*

Just between God & me:

1. What do you aspire to? Do you think you can achieve it with God's help?

_____

_____

_____

_____

_____

_____

_____

2. Are you certain your dreams are in line with God's plan for you?

_____

_____

_____

_____

_____

_____

_____

_____

_____

_____

_____

3. How do you plan to keep God in the center of pursuing your goals?

_____

_____

_____

_____

_____

_____

_____

_____

_____

_____

_____

_____

_____

Thoughts I can share with my group:

_____

_____

_____

_____

_____

_____

_____

_____

_____

_____

_____

_____

_____

_____

_____

_____

_____

_____

_____

_____

_____

_____

_____

_____

_____

_____

_____

_____

_____

_____

_____

Renewing My Trust

Day 2 - I Tell You the Truth

Repetition is a wonderful thing! When my calendar alarm pops up on my screen, I put it on snooze, and it pops up again in a few minutes. I need that! I need repetition for the idea to sink in. A repeated message reminds us, reinforces, and confirms what we first heard.

Our Lord Jesus, rabbi and great teacher, knew we would have a hard time believing Him. His messages were revolutionary to the status quo back then and they still are today!

In the Book of John, Jesus repeatedly said then and says to us now,

John 3:3   I tell you the **truth**

John 3:5   I tell you the **truth**

John 3: 10 I tell you the **truth**

John 5:19   I tell you the **truth**

John 5:25   I tell you the **truth**

John 6:26   I tell you the **truth**

John 6:47   I tell you the **truth**,
            the one who believes
            has eternal life

Pilate, I believe, was cynical when he retorted to Jesus, **"What is truth?"** (John 18:38). Hardened by his allegiance to Rome and by his disappointing assignment in remote Judea, his vocation was not feeding his ego. And when Pilate found himself face to face with the Son of God, his spiritual blindness prevented him from seeing that Jesus is **"the Way, the Truth, and the Life,"** (John 14:6).

When Jesus says to us through His Word, *"I tell you the truth"* He is reaching right into my heart and yours with love beyond comprehension.

He isn't expressing a political view or giving us a sales pitch. His truth is not about money or power as in other religions. It's not to make us slaves or have a stronghold over our lives.

The truth that Jesus brings is dependable, completely honest, and it protects us from lies. His purpose is our redemption; now and through eternity!

His truth is pure love.

"The Lord is near to all who call on him, to all who call on him in truth," (Psalm 145:18).

"But when he, the Spirit of truth, comes, he will guide you into all the truth," (John 16:13).

Just between God & me:

1. Was there a time when you were cynical about the word of God? What were the circumstances?

_____

_____

_____

_____

_____

_____

_____

2. When seeing Jesus say, "I tell you the truth" over and over again, what is your response? Why?

_____

_____

_____

_____

_____

_____

_____

_____

_____

_____

_____

_____

3. How do you plan to learn more about God's truth?

_____

_____

_____

_____

_____

_____

_____

_____

_____

_____

_____

_____

Thoughts I can share with my group:

_____

_____

_____

_____

_____

_____

_____

_____

_____

_____

_____

_____

_____

_____

_____

_____

_____

_____

_____

_____

_____

_____

_____

_____

_____

_____

_____

_____

Getting the Tangles Out

Day 3 - Looking Back

One of my goals is to embrace change as my friend. Tough goal, wouldn't you say? I know if I can adjust my D.R.A.'s (dirty rotten attitudes), I won't be tempted to battle change as much. Even though a consistently changing world is a certainty, we have the assurance that *"Jesus Christ is the same yesterday and today and forever,"* (Hebrews 13:8).

One thing we tend to do is rewind the memory of past events— of how God worked through our lives for His glory, and why not? We love to tell them over and over and over again. My pastor once quipped, "It seems the older we get, the better we were." Did you ever get an award, win a prize, get your name printed in the news, be successful in sports, or get applause for a performance? You might even have an engraved plaque hanging on the wall, or stuck in a closet, but it's there— a reminder that God has done something wonderful in your life!

We also remember the sorrowful events over and over and over again. Did someone else get an award that you thought should have been yours? Did you lose a contest, miss getting some recognition, get dropped from a team, or turned down after an audition? Have you or a loved one ever dealt with a serious illness, death, or been in great financial distress? Only time can soften the pain of those memories, but we still remember.

God didn't intend for us to keep looking back. That's a sure recipe for discouragement and for comparing ourselves to others. It's good that we're not quite the same as we were back then. We're better for having a lot more experience and I hope much stronger in the Word!

Let God give you a new beginning. Ask Him through prayer how to best serve Him today! Whether successful, broken, or both, let God repurpose your life—all for His glory.

THE RE-PURPOSED LIFE

God can take your brokenness and give you a new beginning!

Won't you let Him?

"*Now to him who is able to do immeasurably more than all we ask or imagine, according to his power that is at work within us, to him be glory in the church and in Christ Jesus throughout all generations, forever and ever. Amen.*" (Ephesians 3:20-21).

Carole Brewer

Just between God & me:

1. What kinds of disappointments have stopped you from setting new goals?

   _____

   _____

   _____

   _____

   _____

   _____

   _____

2. Name the people who discourage you as you try to be a follower of Jesus Christ? In what ways can you have victory over the discouragement?

   _____

   _____

   _____

   _____

   _____

   _____

   _____

3. Since we serve God in the present, what has He laid on your heart to do for Him this year?

   _____

   _____

   _____

   _____

   _____

   _____

   _____

Thoughts I can share with my group:

_____

_____

_____

_____

_____

_____

_____

_____

_____

_____

_____

_____

_____

_____

_____

_____

_____

_____

_____

_____

_____

_____

_____

_____

_____

_____

_____

_____

_____

_____

_____

Rediscovering Me

Day 4 - Being Liked

Have you ever been desperate for people to like you? Thinking back to my pre-Christian days, I remember feeling if I could only be a member of that club or have that car or live on that street, then people would like me. I did get applause for my performance in a musical, boosting my self-esteem from a *minus 10* to a *minus 5*. It was an improvement but not a lasting one. After learning grooming tips through a modeling course, my lack of confidence still hurt my attempts to audition, do well on job interviews, and relax when meeting new people. It was a painful, confusing time in my early adult life but it was my pain, and I was going to exercise my prideful right to hang on to it.

When striving to be "liked" by others, people with low self-esteem often give into peer and family pressure. Criticism, even if constructive, can be taken as a slap. The great fear of rejection especially interferes with the giving and receiving of love.

Jesus understands.

"...He had no beauty or majesty to attract us to him, nothing in his appearance that we should desire him. He was despised and rejected by mankind, a man of suffering, and familiar with pain. Like one from whom people hide their faces he was despised, and we held him in low esteem. Surely he took up our pain and bore our suffering," (Isaiah 53:2-4).

Even women who know the Lord struggle with trading self-esteem for Christ-esteem. It's a spiritual battle that requires full surrender to the Holy Spirit living within us. (Ephesians, Chapter 6)

In the Book of Romans, Paul confirms,

"...we know that suffering produces perseverance; perseverance, character; and character, hope. And hope does not put us to shame, because God's love has been poured out into our hearts through the Holy Spirit, who has been given to us," (Romans 5:3-5).

Through Christ's sacrifice for us, we are far beyond being liked. (John 15:13) We are totally and unconditionally approved of, loved, and accepted by God. Jesus desires to be our closest and most intimate friend.

Just between God & me:

1. What kinds of things do you do to be liked by others?

_____

_____

_____

_____

_____

_____

_____

_____

_____

_____

_____

_____

_____

_____

2. Have you ever struggled with low self-esteem in the past?

_____

_____

_____

_____

_____

_____

_____

3. Do you honestly still battle with feeling your value is less than others? What do you think keeps you from escaping this form of bondage?

_____

_____

_____

_____

_____

_____

_____

_____

4. In what ways can you encourage others to walk in the security and love we receive from Jesus?

_____

_____

_____

_____

_____

_____

_____

_____

Thoughts I can share with my group:

_____
_____
_____
_____
_____
_____
_____
_____
_____
_____
_____
_____
_____
_____
_____
_____
_____
_____
_____
_____
_____
_____
_____
_____
_____
_____
_____
_____
_____

Day 5 - Surrender Pray Arise

SURRENDER

✟ I will ask God to help me to pursue a dream aligned with His will.

My thoughts _____

_____

✟ As I read God's Word, I will depend on the Spirit of Truth to guide me in all truth.

My thoughts _____

_____

✝ I will embrace the new beginning God has for me today and look for new ways to serve Him.

My thoughts _____

_____

✝ I will trade my self-esteem for Christ-esteem.

My thoughts _____

_____

Now, take time to bathe in God's presence:

PRAY

ADORATION : expressing my love
Proclaiming God's magnificence by speaking His attributes and singing His praises. (i.e. His greatness, goodness, glory, love)

CONFESSION : admitting my sin
My thoughts and deeds that have dishonored God:

PRAYER PROMPT

I confess that I internalize messages that are not from You and that I don't take time each day to listen to Your voice.

SUPPLICATION: asking God to help me
(i.e. health, responsibilities, time-stretching, peace, restored joy)

INTERCESSION: asking God to help others
(i.e. health, responsibilities, time-stretching, peace, restored joy)
Standing in the gap for those who don't know God

THANKSGIVING: expressing deepest gratitude
Speaking and singing from my heart.

ARISE

"For I know the plans I have for you," declares the Lord, "plans to prosper you and not to harm you, plans to give you hope and a future," (Jeremiah 29:11).

A Song to Bless

Your Love Lives On

Words & Music by Carole Brewer

Captured in the wonder, in awe of Your glory
You have made each living thing
I can feel Your presence, Your Spirit here inside me
Peace beyond my understanding.

Lord God, Creator of love
Come and fill up my life with Your song
You're here; there's nothing to fear
For I know in my heart that Your love lives on.

Freed from all the darkness and touched by Your glory
You have changed the very heart of me,
the heart of me
Not for just an instant and longer than a lifetime
Grace throughout eternity

Oh, Lord God, Creator of love
Come and fill up my life with Your song,
Your song
You're here; there's nothing to fear
For I know in my heart that Your love lives on.

Week Five

Another New Beginning

Enlighten Up

DAY 1 – Getting Whacked

Picture a group of our fifty high school girls standing lopsided on a lumpy grass field wearing team bibs over blue snap-up gym suits and daydreaming. That was my PE class!

Lynn played center on my field hockey team and I stood directly behind her. On the count of three, Lynn would hopefully whack the hockey puck to the left before her opponent could whack it to the right.

The whistle blew and the two center whackers yelled, "One! Two!" Up and down their sticks clicked. Then, "Three!" Mimicking a golfer, Lynn not only hit the puck to the left but continued through her stroke, swinging around to hit the left side of my nose. Ouch!

Seeing me drop to the field, our teacher raced to my side finding me stunned but okay. Another player, relieved to be excused from class, accompanied me to the nurse's office where a doctor's appointment was promptly scheduled.

Within a few hours, a doctor was pulling and tweaking my cheeks to the right and left of my nose, asking, "Does this hurt? Does that hurt?" "Yes," I answered. It hurt! He determined there were no broken bones but my high school field hockey experience caused my nose to angle slightly to the right.

About five years later, I was driving to my college class and for a second, took my eyes off the road. No texting back then but the distraction caused me to slide into the bumper of a car that abruptly stopped in front of me. I was whacked again! My face hit the steering wheel and my slightly angled-to-the-right nose was permanently moved back to center!

In life, whacks happen; first to the left and then to the right. Considering the difficult and stressful times we now live in, most of us seldom have whack-less days.

Does this hurt?

Does that hurt?

Yes, it hurts!

Whether hit from the side or hit from a full-circle swing, we are tempted to take our eyes off of God and His perfect plan for us.

Be encouraged, dear friend! With each whack, I know I can go back to God's Word and get re-aligned with Him. He not only straightens my angled days back to the center of His will but gives me an extra portion of His grace and peace.

"Consider it a sheer gift, friends, when tests and challenges come at you from all sides. You know that under pressure, your faith-life is forced into the open and shows its true colors. So don't try to get out of anything prematurely. Let it do its work so you become mature and well-developed, not deficient in any way," (James 1:2-4 MSG).

Just between God & me:

1. Name a life-experience when you really felt *whacked*! Did you run away from it, confront it on your own, or face it with God's help?

_____

_____

_____

_____

_____

2. Looking back, did you consider your situation from a worldly perspective? How do you view that situation now?

_____

_____

_____

_____

_____

_____

3. How do you plan to prepare for future *whacks* that are certain to come our way?

_____

_____

_____

_____

_____

_____

Thoughts I can share with my group:

_____

_____

_____

_____

_____

_____

_____

_____

_____

_____

_____

_____

_____

_____

_____

_____

_____

_____

_____

_____

_____

_____

_____

_____

_____

_____

_____

_____

_____

_____

_____

Renewing My Trust

DAY 2 - Trustworthy Love

When I was in high school my youth group took several trips including a weekend getaway to San Francisco. It wasn't a missions trip by any stretch of the imagination. Our only mission was to have fun; it was the mission of our chaperones as well. Where were they?! I'm not sure; but it was late at night and around five of us girls decided to leave our hotel rooms to go down to the street. Looking back, I'm asking myself how naïve could we have been to walk around a strange city— so vulnerable?

Just around the corner from our hotel, a few of young men spotted us and headed toward us. We made a frightful dash for our school bus in the hotel parking lot. Amazingly, we were able to pry open the door, get in, and shut it just before the men arrived. We were terrified as they yelled at us and banged on the bus windows. Then there was a distraction; two ladies-of-the-night caught their eyes, and they abandoned us to follow them.

I knew nothing of God's Word but I did sense the presence of a protector. God knew me and was shielding me from harm even if I didn't acknowledge Him. It's as if He was saying to me, "Carole, turn around and pay attention. I'm your Lord. I'm here for you, and I love you." With no knowledge of the Source of those gentle encounters, I simply brushed them off.

I now know His love for me, demonstrated that night and many other times in my pre-Christian life, is trustworthy.

"When I said, "My foot is slipping," your unfailing love, Lord, supported me," (Psalm 94:18).

When you walk, your steps will not be hampered
Proverbs 4:12

The Lord makes firm the steps of the one
who delights in him
Psalm 37:23

My steps have held to your paths;
my feet have not stumbled
Psalm 17:5

Just between God & me:

1. Have you ever naively put yourself in a dangerous situation thinking it was just for fun? If so, were you able to recognize God's love and protection for you in that circumstance? Why or why not? How do you view that past situation now?

_____

_____

_____

_____

_____

_____

2. How has God shown you personally that His love for you is trustworthy?

_____

_____

_____

_____

_____

_____

3. It what ways can you demonstrate your trustworthiness to others?

_____

_____

_____

_____

_____

_____

_____

Thoughts I can share with my group:

_____

_____

_____

_____

_____

_____

_____

_____

_____

_____

_____

_____

_____

_____

_____

_____

_____

_____

_____

Getting the Tangles Out

DAY 3 Word Smart - Open Heart

A great disadvantage for me growing up was that I knew nothing about the Bible. I didn't even know there was a New Testament. I thought the whole book was old!

As an adult and new believer, my enthusiasm was overflowing. I'd say, "She's a Christian!" with such excitement believing when a woman defined herself as Christian (*little Christ*), she was a true follower of Jesus. I would be shocked when meeting someone whose actions didn't support her claimed Christian identity. Seeing this as a new believer flustered me. Over the years, though, I'm sure many things I've said or done have caused others to be flustered and wondering if I truly believe.

Spending hours in the Bible and producing correct answers to study questions will confirm an individual is Word smart. My question is, for all of us, has the gathering of information into our brains also transferred to our hearts? Hearing and knowing are not the same as living and doing. Jesus' brother James tells us,

"Do not merely listen to the word, and so deceive yourselves. Do what it says," (James 1:22).

The Book of Acts records

"When they saw the courage of Peter and John and realized that they were unschooled, ordinary men, they were astonished and they took note that these men had been with Jesus," (Acts 4:13).

Being with Jesus is the key! Being His hands, His feet, and perhaps the only "Jesus" others will ever see, is the opportunity we have to live out the Gospel and bring God glory.

Just between God & me:

1. Describe your impression of the phrase "hearing and knowing are not the same as living and doing."

    _____

    _____

    _____

    _____

    _____

    _____

2. What actions can you take today to demonstrate you are a follower of Jesus? Will your actions differ from the way you approached things in the past? How?

    _____

    _____

    _____

    _____

    _____

    _____

3. List more ways you can reflect the love of Jesus to others.

    _____

    _____

    _____

    _____

    _____

    _____

Thoughts I can share with my group:

_____
_____
_____
_____
_____
_____
_____
_____
_____
_____
_____
_____
_____
_____
_____
_____
_____
_____
_____
_____
_____
_____
_____
_____
_____
_____
_____
_____
_____

Rediscovering Me

DAY 4 - Wedges

Think of the Lord and how He is always ready to welcome us with open arms. Don't you want to run into His embrace and linger there in a heart to heart hug?

Imagine now a wedge placed in the middle of that hug preventing our hearts from making direct contact with the Lord's heartbeat.

- Fear
- Anger
- Depression
- Jealousy
- Self-pity
- Judging others
- Boredom
- Greed
- Impatience
- Arrogance

...that keep us farther away from the heart of Jesus

All wedges (sin) are ultimately directed toward God and they block our access to His treasures. Chiseling them out requires a change in both our heads and our hearts.

Another wedge to consider is gossip; it's a very subtle sin. One might say, "I can't tell you how much I respect so and so for how well she is handling ALL that's she's going in her life right now. She's not only dealing with this problem, but she has that problem, another problem, something else has come up, and she's enduring huge problem over there. I thought you should know everything so you'll know how to pray for her."

Social networking, tabloids, talk-shows, news reports, reality TV, some blogs, and text messaging demonstrate our culture has developed a ravenous appetite for details about the misery and misfortune of others.

Please hear my heart. If we're not part of the problem or part of the solution, it's gossip! Stay close to the heart of Jesus; and, for the sake of others, be a trustworthy friend who can keep a secret.

"If you belong to Christ, then you are Abraham's seed, and heirs according to the promise," (Galatians 3:29).

A woman choosing to live as an heiress in God's Kingdom will ask God to help her replace the wedges in her life with the fruits of the Holy Spirit. (Galatians 5:22)

Love - Joy - Peace - Patience - Kindness

Goodness - Faithfulness - Gentleness - Self-control

As we daily demonstrate these God-given attributes, the beauty of Christ will surely shine through us.

Just between God & me:

1. What wedges have caused your heart to be out of sync with the heart of Jesus?

_____

_____

_____

_____

_____

_____

_____

2. Are you holding onto wedges you thought were harmless or insignificant? How do you plan to chisel them out of your daily life?

_____

_____

_____

_____

_____

_____

_____

3. Is gossip a habit you've learned from friends, family members, or co-workers? Can you think of ways to change your conversation from idle talk and rumors to words that honor God?

_____

_____

_____

_____

_____

_____

_____

4. Do you know anyone who demonstrates the fruits of the Holy Spirit in her life? What things has she done to make you notice?

_____

_____

_____

_____

_____

_____

Thoughts I can share with my group:

_____

_____

_____

_____

_____

_____

_____

_____

_____

_____

_____

_____

_____

_____

_____

_____

_____

_____

_____

Day 5 - Surrender Pray Arise

SURRENDER

✝ I realize that sometimes it takes a good "whack" to get me back into alignment with Jesus

My thoughts _____

_____

✝ God loves me and is watching over me even when I'm not aware of His presence.

My thoughts _____

_____

✝ Memorizing and studying God's Word has limited results unless I actually embrace His Word and live it out.

My thoughts _____

_____

✝ The wedges in my life interfere with my heart to heart relationship with Jesus.

My thoughts _____

_____

PRAY

ADORATION : expressing my love
Proclaiming God's magnificence by speaking His attributes and singing His praises. (i.e. His greatness, goodness, glory, love)

CONFESSION : admitting my sin
My thoughts and deeds that have dishonored God:

PRAYER PROMPT

*I confess that I'm grateful for the prayers of others
when I am too numb to pray.*

SUPPLICATION: asking God to help me
(i.e. health, responsibilities, time-stretching, peace, restored joy)

INTERCESSION: asking God to help others
(i.e., health, responsibilities, time-stretching, peace, restored joy)
Standing in the gap for those who don't know God

THANKSGIVING: expressing deepest gratitude
Speaking and singing from my heart

ARISE

For in him we live, move, and have our being.
Acts 17:28

*...but those who hope in the Lord
will renew their strength.
They will soar on wings like eagles;
they will run and not grow weary,
they will walk and not be faint.*
Isaiah 40:31

A Song to Bless

Child of the Promise

Words & Music by Carole Brewer

(Inspired by Galatians 3:29)

I praise the Lord for all His mercy
I praise the Lord for all that will be
I praise Him for His unfailing love
For His faithfulness to me
I rejoice to know of His presence
I rejoice to know that He has set me free
I rejoice to know of His greatest gift
Of His promises to me

Oh, I am a child of the promise, an offspring of Abraham
An heir with Christ my Savior
The King of who I am
Yes, and I am a new creation
Redeemed by the blood of the Lamb
I will live my life for Jesus Christ
My promise is in Him

The promise is for all of my family
For all of my loved ones far away
Let me shine the light of my Jesus Christ
So they will join me and say

Oh, I am a child of the promise, an offspring of Abraham
An heir with Christ my Savior
He's the King of who I am
Yes, and I am a new creation
Redeemed by the blood of the Lamb
I will live my life for Jesus Christ
My promise is in Him

Week Six

Another New Beginning

Enlighten Up

DAY 1 – In-flight Witnessing

Recently I had the opportunity to fly on one of those cool little turboprop jets—the ones that fly lower and slower but give passengers a better view of the scenery. Of course the interior was cramped with two scaled-down seats on each side of the aisle. In such cases, relating in some way to the person adjacent to you is inevitable.

Having the window seat and feeling very blessed, I was ready and waiting to share my faith with whomever God would seat next to me.

A pleasant looking man showed up and fastened his seatbelt. We took off! Then he immediately retrieved a small book from his carry-on. While enjoying my view, I did notice my row-mate reading a few lines, closing his book, looking up, and repeating the process. What was he studying? My curiosity got the best of me and I strained, with my not-so-good vision on the left, to see the cover. Even with his napkin slightly over the corner of the book, I determined that the title was Rules of God. Rules of God? What would that be about? Was this man a pastor or an elder? What church? Hmm. Oh good, here's my chance!

When the beverage service came, he handed over to me the peanuts and my cup of tea. I said, "Thank you," and waited about 30 seconds for my overture. "That little book you're reading intrigues me. What's it about?" He lit up and enthusiastically displayed the cover of his book titled Rules of Golf!

For the remainder of the flight, this friendly golf pro explained to me with numerous diagrams and photos a variety of obscure rules that especially apply to the famous St. Andrews Golf Course in Scotland. How educational for me!

I guess I could've interjected, "Do you pray before you putt?' But the flaps were down, and our plane was landing. When on my own again in the terminal, I could barely stop laughing!

There'll be other chances, so let's be ready to share what God has done for us! Here are some *how-to's* direct from God's Word!

"Be wise in the way you act toward outsiders; make the most of every opportunity. Let your conversation be always full of grace, seasoned with salt, so that you may know how to answer everyone." (Colossians 4:5-6).

"But in your hearts revere Christ as Lord. Always be prepared to give an answer to everyone who asks you to give the reason for the hope that you have. But do this with gentleness and respect," (1 Peter 3:15).

Just between God & me:

1. How would you describe your comfort level when sharing your faith with strangers? Are you enthusiastic and ready or do you feel intimidated because of our changing culture?

   _____

   _____

   _____

   _____

   _____

   _____

   _____

2. Have you ever had the opportunity to share your faith with a stranger while in transit? If so, what happened?

_____
_____
_____
_____
_____
_____
_____
_____
_____
_____

3. In what ways can you plan ahead for sharing your faith with others?

_____
_____
_____
_____
_____
_____
_____
_____
_____
_____

Thoughts I can share with my group:

_____
_____
_____
_____
_____
_____
_____
_____
_____
_____
_____
_____
_____
_____
_____
_____
_____
_____
_____
_____
_____
_____
_____
_____
_____
_____
_____
_____
_____

Renewing My Trust

DAY 2 - Faith Reaffirmed

When Jesus walked on earth, He gave forgiveness and the promise of abundant and eternal life equally to men and women. How radical for those times. Women actively supported Jesus' ministry, and He was their friend; He spoke with women, healed women, and chose a woman to be the first to see Him after rising from the grave. Such love and respect for women by a Jewish man of that time was unheard of. Whether then or now, Jesus' love for us is unchanging.

With such an intimate Friend, isn't it natural to want to know as much about Jesus as we can? Though He is God and we are not, we can find many synonyms for Jesus in the Bible that help us know Him better. In fact, you'll find 226 names for Jesus in your Bible Concordance. Here are some of my favorites:

Anointed of the Lord	*Psalms 2:2*
Counselor	*Isaiah 9:6*
Deliverer	*Romans 11:26*
Faithful and True	*Revelation 19:11*
Holy Servant	*Acts 4:27*
Image of the Invisible God	*Colossians 1:15*
King over all the earth	*Zechariah 14:19*
Light of the world	*John 9:5*

Physician	*Luke 4:23*
Prince of peace	*Isaiah 9:6*
Source of Eternal Salvation	*Hebrews 5:9*
Teacher	*Mark 12:14*

With the lifeline of God's Holy Word and the presence of His Holy Spirit, He gives us the strength to revitalize even after extreme challenges. He will never let us go.

Believe!

Jesus is

"the stone you builders rejected, which has become the cornerstone.' Salvation is found in no one else, for there is no other name under heaven given to mankind by which we must be saved," (Acts 4:11-12).

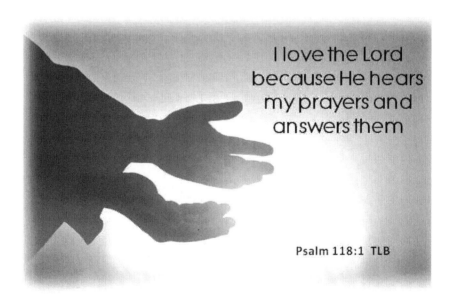

I love the Lord because He hears my prayers and answers them

Psalm 118:1 TLB

Carole Brewer

Just between God & me:

Statement of Faith: Write "Yes, I agree" along with additional comments you may have.

I am confident that the Bible is the holy inspired Word of God.

_____

_____

_____

_____

I acknowledge and honor God, my heavenly Father, Creator of Heaven and Earth. His love is infinitely perfect.

_____

_____

_____

_____

I proclaim Jesus Christ as my Lord—the Son of God who came in human flesh—the King of my life and heart whom I give all glory, honor, and praise.

_____

_____

_____

_____

I embrace the Holy Spirit as the third person of the Godhead (Trinity). I depend on the Holy Spirit for guidance, comfort, and empowerment to serve God—demonstrating the love of Jesus to others in my daily life.

_____

_____

_____

_____

I believe that Adam's fall into sin left humanity without the hope of heaven apart from a new birth. This new birth was made possible by Jesus Christ's death and bodily resurrection.

_____

_____

_____

_____

I believe the offer of salvation is God's love-gift to all. Those who accept it by faith, apart from works, become new creatures in Christ.

_____

_____

_____

_____

Thoughts I can share with my group:

_____

_____

_____

_____

_____

_____

_____

_____

_____

_____

_____

_____

_____

_____

_____

_____

_____

_____

_____

_____

_____

_____

_____

_____

_____

_____

_____

_____

_____

_____

Getting the Tangles Out

DAY 3 - Empowered

One of the most important gifts God gives us is His presence. Have you felt it? Are you aware of it? In His presence we have the power to love the unlovable, endure hardships without completely breaking, make tough God-honoring choices, and do many things we think we can't.

Even when I've been numb with grief and loss, I knew God was with me. In some cases, I could feel the hairs on my arms stand up, or get a quick chill, or utter words in prayer without understanding them. I've felt a warmth and a presence that is irreplaceable and have been calm and at peace in times when it made no sense. (Philippians 4:7).

Should it be a surprise? God told us in His Word, *"Never will I leave you; never will I forsake you,"* **(Hebrews 13:5)**; He keeps His promises.

Before leaving earth Jesus told His disciples to expect the Comforter to come; He has! The Holy Spirit, also known as Advocate, Comforter, Counselor, and Holy Ghost, is the unseen Spirit of God. When the Disciples were empowered, they documented their experiences so we too could know the miraculous, glorious truth. How sad for those who don't believe.

*A closed mind and
a heart hardened to the Gospel
are the enemy's trophies.*

At the moment we decide to follow Jesus, the Holy Spirit takes residence in our being. The Apostle Paul confirms this saying,

> *"Do you not know that your bodies are temples of the Holy Spirit, who is in you, whom you have received from God? You are not your own,"* (1 Corinthians 6:19).

Jesus said,

> *"If you love me, keep my commands. And I will ask the Father, and he will give you another advocate to help you and be with you forever—the Spirit of truth,"* (John 14:15-17).

The Holy Spirit works in our lives to free us from faith entanglers. Surrendering to His will is the best way to get back on our feet, give the enemy a "black eye," and live victoriously in Christ!

Here are some of the tough choices that God, through His Spirit, empowers us to make:

- *Desire God more than things*
- *Keep sex within marriage*
- *Manage finances with integrity*

The Holy Spirit also empowers us to be extravagant with kindness and look for ways to share with others the love that Christ has lavished upon us. Serving God revitalizes our faith when we see how He can use us for His greater purposes.

"May the God of hope fill you with all joy and peace as you trust in him, so that you may overflow with hope by the power of the Holy Spirit," (Romans 15:13).

"Finally, be strong in the Lord and in his mighty power," (Ephesians 6:10).

Just between God & me:

1. Can you think of a specific time when you felt God's presence and power working in your life? Explain what happened.

_____

_____

_____

_____

_____

_____

_____

_____

2. Even as a Christian, have you ever made important decisions without taking time to ask the Holy Spirit for wisdom and direction? If so, why do you think you neglected to ask?

_____

_____

_____

_____

_____

_____

_____

_____

3. On difficult days, do you instinctively ask the Holy Spirit to replace your anxiety with peace and wisdom? If not, what will help you remember to ask in the future?

_____

_____

_____

_____

_____

_____

_____

_____

_____

_____

4. Do you need help from the Holy Spirit today? If so, pray now. Father God, through Your Holy Spirit, please give me Your wisdom, strength, and peace as I face this difficult situation. Thank you for hearing my prayers and for meeting all my needs. In Jesus' name, Amen.

_____

_____

_____

_____

_____

_____

_____

_____

_____

_____

Thoughts I can share with my group:

_____
_____
_____
_____
_____
_____
_____
_____
_____
_____
_____
_____
_____
_____
_____
_____
_____
_____
_____
_____
_____
_____
_____
_____
_____
_____
_____
_____
_____
_____
_____
_____
_____

Rediscovering Me

DAY 4 - A New Life

I'm so grateful that the God we serve gives us second chances over and over again. A single second chance wouldn't be nearly enough for me. I somehow blow it every day.

Paul also confesses saying, *"I do not understand what I do. For what I want to do I do not do, but what I hate I do,"* (Romans 7:15).

But when I say, "Oh Lord, I'm so sorry. Please help me to not do that again", I sense, through the Holy Spirit, the presence of the Living God. He opens His loving arms to console us, saying, "Come on back. I'm with you. Let's try again." That's the assurance we receive from our forgiving, merciful, loving Savior.

A woman, in Jesus' time on earth, was about to be stoned to death for being in an adulterous affair. The Pharisees, using her situation as bait to trap Jesus, asked, *"Now what do you say?"* Jesus advocated for her by answering, *"Let any one of you who is without sin be the first to throw a stone at her."* One by one, the men departed from the scene. *"…with the woman still standing there. Jesus … asked her, "Woman, where are they? Has no one condemned you?" "No one, sir," she said. "Then neither do I condemn you," Jesus declared. "Go now and leave your life of sin,"* (John 8:3-11).

Jesus gives us the same new beginning that he gave the woman 2,000 years ago. Whether large or small, sin is sin and when we're truly sorry, His love and forgiveness make us clean from all unrighteousness. (1 John 1:9) We have another chance!

The dictionary states that life is the opposite of death; along with a long list of other definitions. I prefer the synonyms since they better describe what "life" looks like. When someone says, "Put some life into it!" what they're saying is, "Put some spirit, animation, brio, dash, esprit, some oomph, verve, vim, and zing into it!" In our case, Jesus gives the best of life and makes it new!

GOD'S WORD DECLARES WHO I AM!

I'm a new creation!

I've been given
a fresh new start!

Christ lives in me!

More love-letters from God:
> *"Therefore, if anyone is in Christ, the new creation has come: The old has gone, the new is here,"* (2 Corinthians 5:17).

> *"We were therefore buried with him through baptism into death in order that, just as Christ was raised from the dead through the glory of the Father, we too may live a new life."* (Romans 6:4).

Carole Brewer

"Take delight in the Lord, and he will give you the desires of your heart," (Psalm 37:4).

"For no word from God will ever fail," (Luke 6:23).

Galatians 2:20-21 from The Message says it this way.

"What actually took place is this: I tried keeping rules and working my head off to please God, and it didn't work. So I quit being a "law woman" so that I could be God's woman. Christ's life showed me how, and enabled me to do it. I identified myself completely with him. Indeed, I have been crucified with Christ. My ego is no longer central. It is no longer important that I appear righteous before you or have your good opinion, and I am no longer driven to impress God. Christ lives in me. The life you see me living is not "mine," but it is lived by faith in the Son of God, who loved me and gave himself for me. I am not going to go back on that."

Have you said, "Yes Lord" to His new call upon your heart? My prayer for all of us is that we walk each day in newness of life with Him.

Just between God & me:

1. What second chances from God have you received in your life?

    _____

    _____

    _____

    _____

    _____

    _____

    _____

2. The accused woman addressed Jesus as sir. Do you come into His presence with the same awe and respect?

_____

_____

_____

_____

_____

_____

_____

3. How does the promise of a new life strengthen your faith and refresh your Spirit?

_____

_____

_____

_____

_____

_____

_____

4. What have you personally experienced as a result of your prayer time these past six weeks?

_____

_____

_____

_____

_____

_____

_____

5. What is your plan to continue spending time in God's presence on a weekly basis?

_____

_____

_____

_____

_____

_____

_____

_____

6. My Letter of Thanksgiving to Jesus

_____

_____

_____

_____

_____

_____

_____

_____

_____

_____

_____

_____

_____

_____

Perhaps you would even consider going public with your testimony by sharing your story with your church family or in a blog.

Thoughts I can share with my group:

_____
_____
_____
_____
_____
_____
_____
_____
_____
_____
_____
_____
_____
_____
_____
_____
_____
_____
_____
_____
_____
_____
_____
_____
_____
_____
_____
_____
_____
_____
_____
_____
_____

Day 5 - Surrender Pray Arise

SURRENDER

✝ At His prompting, I'll depend on the Holy Spirit to help me tell others, either through words or actions, of the hope I have in Jesus Christ.

My thoughts _____

_____

✝ Knowing the many names of Jesus gives me a window into His character as God's Son, Mighty King, and my closest friend.

My thoughts _____

_____

✝ I will allow the Holy Spirit to help me disentangle the things that bind up my faith and release me to be free in God's presence.

My thoughts _____

_____

✝ God has given me another chance to re-commit my life saying, "Yes Lord! I want to put You first in my life again."

My thoughts _____

_____

PRAY

Taking time to converse with my Father God through Jesus Christ, His Son, and through the Holy Spirit:

ADORATION : expressing my love
Proclaiming God's magnificence by speaking His attributes and singing His praises. (i.e. His greatness, goodness, glory, love)

CONFESSION : admitting my sin
My thoughts and deeds that have dishonored God:

PRAYER PROMPT

Forgive me when I don't spend time talking with You each day on behalf of others and myself.

My Decision to Be a Follower of Jesus Christ

Now is my time. Today is my day!
What once was my life,
I now give away
to You, my Lord Jesus,
my Savior and King!
I give You my heart and my everything.

Poem by Carole Brewer

God Loves You: But God demonstrates His own love toward us, in that while we were still sinners, Christ died for us. —Romans 5:8

All Are Sinners: For all have sinned and fall short of the glory of God. —Romans 3:23

God's Remedy for Sin: But as many as received Him, to them He gave the right to become children of God, to those who believe in His name. —John 1:12

All May Be Saved Now: But these are written that you may believe that Jesus is the Christ, the Son of God, and that believing you may have life in His name. —John 20:31

Receive Christ as Your Savior Now: Confessing to God that I am a sinner, and believing that the Lord Jesus Christ died for my sins on the cross and was raised for my justification, I now receive and confess Him as my personal Savior.

Name: _____   Date: _____

Assurance from Jesus: Most assuredly, I say to you, he who hears My word and believes in Him who sent Me has everlasting life, and shall not come into judgment, but has passed from death into life. —John 5:24

SUPPLICATION: asking God to help me
(i.e. health, responsibilities, time-stretching, peace, restored joy)

INTERCESSION: asking God to help others
(i.e. health, responsibilities, time-stretching, peace, restored joy)
Standing in the gap for those who don't know God

THANKSGIVING: expressing deepest gratitude
Speaking and singing from my heart

ARISE

You did it: you changed wild lament into whirling dance;
You ripped off my black mourning band
and decked me with wildflowers.
I'm about to burst with song;
I can't keep quiet about you.
God, my God,
I can't thank you enough.
Psalm 30:11-12 MSG

A Song to Bless

New Life

Words & Music by Carole Brewer

A new beginning, a fresh new start
Another chance to change my heart
I'm a new creation born of God
Filled with His Spirit and love

New life, a new life
I've given Him my heart,
and He's given to me a new life
The past has passed, and I'm moving on to new life

Another trial and there's more pain
But Jesus is walking me through again
His yoke is easy, His burden light
And I'm walking by faith, not by sight

Into life, a new life
I've given Him my heart,
and He's given to me a new life
The past has passed, and I'm moving on…

Through His eyes I clearly see
And those memories, those memories
Have no hold over me
Jesus gives me His strength
He gives me peace, perfect peace

And a new beginning, a fresh new start
Another chance to change my heart
I'm a new creation born of God
Filled with His Spirit and love

New life, a new life
I've given Him my heart,
and He's given to me a new life
The past has passed, and I'm moving on
I'm free a last and I'm moving on
The past has passed, and I'm moving on
to new life in Christ

How to Use this Book

*R*evitalize is divided into six weeks with five devotionals per week. You can also choose to go straight through as a 30-day devotional.

Depending on your work week, assign your starting day. Do make sure, whether you're in this book or not, to take your Sabbath rest. God ordains it and it's so important for our spiritual health.

During the six weeks, each of the five days has the same recurring theme:

- ○ **Enlighten Up**
- ○ **Renewing My Trust**
- ○ **Getting the Tangles Out**
- ○ **Rediscovering Me**
- ○ **A SPA for My Heart**

Days 1 through 4 will give you a chance to write your personal thoughts about the questions I've placed under the heading **Just between God and me:**

If you're going through this devotional with a group, add the comments you feel comfortable sharing under **Thoughts for sharing with others:**

Whether with your group, in a blog post, or sharing on social networking, the insights you gain can be used by God in a powerful way to make a difference in someone else's life.

DAY 5- A SPA for My Heart is your time to be alone with God.

Here are the sections:

SURRENDER – a time to remember the points made in the previous four lessons and your responses to the questions. Add into your prayer time the topics and Scriptures that have especially resonated with you.

PRAY - Find a quiet place to spend time in God's presence. Treasure your personal visits knowing that Jesus, both Most High King and Shepherd of Souls will be listening to your every word as you share your praise and petitions with Him.

On Day 5 of every week, the order of prayer includes Adoration, Confession, Supplication, Intercession, and Thanksgiving. It will be a helpful guide but please remember there are no set rules for talking with God. Sincere prayers from your heart are what matter most. Let the Holy Spirit direct your conversation.

ARISE – With God's peace that passes all understanding, move into your daily life knowing He is always with you.

Just a note about the graphics: I've placed key photos from my Revitalize presentations throughout this book in hopes that they clearly speak to visual learners.

Then to end each week, I'm blessed to share one of my original songs. My lyrics are in poetic form to encourage you and confirm God's presence and power in your life.

Carole Brewer

Suggestions for Group Leaders

Thank you for leading Revitalize as a group study! Here are some ideas for structuring your time together:

- Plan a weekly gathering over a six-week period.

- Depending on the number of attendees, divide into small groups of 4-8 around each table or a circle of chairs.

- At the first meeting, let each woman share a little about herself in her small group—2-3 minutes per person. (i.e. name, where she's from, vocation, hobbies, etc.)

- Begin each session with 10 minutes of singing songs of praise and worship. Ask someone to lead using guitar, piano, or pre-recorded accompaniment tracks.

- Each week, play **A Song to Bless** using your computer or phone with speakers the group can hear. Go to YouTube.com and put in the link for that week listed on Pg. 142. Song downloads are also available for purchase on Amazon.com.

- Take time for praise reports, prayer requests, and prayer.

- Re-read or paraphrase the lessons for the week and comment on the Scripture references.

- Because there will be many personal answers under the title **"Just Between God and Me"**, some participants may not prefer to bring their books to the group meeting. Handouts will provide a safe way for the ladies to bring their notes each week.

Download the FREE Revitalize group handouts

@ http://www.carolebrewer.com/womens-events

Scripture References

Week One	Week Two	Week Three
Proverbs 3:5-6 MSG	Proverbs 17:22	Psalm 126:2
Psalm 16:11	2 Timothy 4:3-5	Genesis 3:1-4
1 Peter 5:8	Ephesians 4:14	2 Corinthians 11:14
Ephesians 6:12, 17	Philippians 4:8	John 4: 16-18
Daniel 10:21	Mark 4:3-9	Colossians 2:2-4
2 Timothy 3:16-17	Colossians 2: 6-7	Romans 8:1
John 16:33	Luke 19:1-9	Romans 12:11-13
Hebrews 1:12	Romans 3:22-24	John 15:5
1 Peter 5:7	Proverbs 18:10 NKJV	Revelation 21:6
Psalm 34:8	Hebrews 4:6	Galatians 6:4
Matthew 5:8	Ephesians 5:14	Jeremiah 29:13-14
John 13:6-9	Nehemiah 8:10	Romans 5:15
Acts 3:19		Jeremiah 29:12
Proverbs 4:11-12		Psalm 30:12 NASB
Matthew 7:7		Isaiah 60:1
John 8:12		
Week Four	**Week Five**	**Week Six**
Psalm 37:5	James 1:2-4 MSG	Colossians 4:5-6
John 3:3,5,10	Psalm 94:18	Psalms 2:2
John 5:19, 25	Proverbs 4:12	Isaiah 9:6
John 6:26,47	Psalm 37:23	Zechariah 14:19
John 16:13	Psalm 17:5	Mark 12:14

John 18:38	James 1:22	Luke 4:23
John 14:6	Acts 4:13	John 9:5, 14:6
Hebrews 13:8	Galatians 3:29, 5:22	Acts 4:27
Ephesians 3:20-21	Jeremiah 29:12	Romans 11:26
Isaiah 53:2-4	Psalm 116:1 TLB	2 Corinthians 9:15
Ephesians 6	Isaiah 40:31	Colossians 1:15,27
Romans 5:3-5	Acts 17:28	Hebrews 5:9
Psalm 145:18		1 Peter 2:26
Jeremiah 29:12		Revelation 19:11
		Acts 4:11-12
		John 6:35, 10:9, 15:1
		John 10:11, 11:25, 14:6
		Philippians 4:7
		Hebrews 13:5
		1 Corinthians 6:19
		John 14: 15-17
		Romans 15:13
		Ephesians 6:10
		Romans 7:15
		John 8:3-11
		1 John 1:9
		2 Corinthians 5:17
		Romans 6:4
		Psalm 37:4
		Luke 6:23
		Galatians 2:20-21 MSG
		Psalm 30:11-12 MSG
About the Author		
1 Corinthians 10:31		
Acts 17:28		

List of Songs by Carole Brewer

Week	Song Title	CD Title
1	I'm Walkin' With My Lord Today	New Life https://www.youtube.com/watch?v=-eq_B9P_QVI
2	Return to Your First Love	New Life https://www.youtube.com/watch?v=EWtF8Hd6_6o
3	Morning Star	Everything Began With You https://www.youtube.com/watch?v=VfH6tguT08Y
4	Your Love Lives On	New Life https://www.youtube.com/watch?v=hG3Dr9fl42I
5	Child of the Promise	New Life https://www.youtube.com/watch?v=yOkiPRwb4mg
6	New Life	New Life https://www.youtube.com/watch?v=3az2tMp3mPA

Carole's wide variety of music styles and songwriting are represented in her four solo albums including **New Life** (Songs of Celebration and Worship), **Everything Began With You** (Timeless Songs of Praise), **The Work of Your Hand** (A Collection of 16 Scripture Songs), and **Celebrate the Lord** (Contemporary Christian Classics). *Servant's Heart/J.W. Brewer Music Publishing Company— Registered with BMI, Broadcast Music, Inc.*

Look for Carole's music and books at:
Amazon.com, iTunes, CD Baby, and CaroleBrewer.com

Carole Brewer

About the Author

Carole **Brewer** is a speaker, author, singer/songwriter, teacher, and radio host who shares Bible-inspired messages with contagious joy. In her daily life, Carole takes to heart, "*Whatever you do-do it all to honor and glorify God,*" (1 Corinthians 10:31).

Education: Carole has a B.A. in Music and an M.A. in Education. She earned four California teaching credentials and has taught classes from First Grade through Adult Education. Carole also holds a diploma in professional modeling. Her Biblical studies include training from Bible Study Fellowship, Community Bible Study, Speak Up With Confidence Seminars, Western Seminary-Sacramento, and Capital Bible College.

Carole's Story: Born cross-eyed and legally blind in her left eye, Carole was ridiculed in elementary school for her outward appearance. Her eye was straightened through surgery at age nine, but Carole lacked the self-confidence and sense of purpose that only a personal relationship with Jesus Christ can bring. During her senior year of college, Carole opened her heart to the truth of God's Word, surrendered to His will, and received her esteem as an heir in Christ. Instead of living with bitterness and discouragement, Carole now walks with Jesus using her God-given talents to share His message of encouragement, hope, and eternal life.

About Carole Brewer Ministries

A full-time teacher in public schools for ten years, Carole began her music ministry in 1998. She became a regular singing guest on Christian television, led worship at conferences, and has been a soloist for churches in Canada, Israel, Germany, Denmark, Iceland, on cruise ships, and in the U.S.

In 2001, Carole began to develop her own presentations for women combining her music with Bible-inspired messages. In fact, many lessons in this book are from keynotes Carole has shared over the last decade.

Carole's greatest joy has been to help women feel loved, experience freedom from past hurts, and understand what it truly means to have their identity in Christ.

Carole offers event planners these popular topics:

- ○ **Revitalize**
- ○ **The King & I**
- ○ **Shopping for a Bargain**
- ○ **Bloom Where You're Planted**
- ○ **Remembering Bethlehem**

...or suggest your own theme.

Learn more @ http://www.carolebrewer.com/womens-events

Carole's ministry has expanded to include a popular radio show called "Bible Chicks". The program features inspiring stories and testimonies that help women strengthen their faith and refresh their spirit. Listen and be blessed by Carole's fabulous guests!

Like us on FaceBook @

BibleChickswithCarole

Listen Now @

BibleChicks.com

"For in him we live, move, and have our being," (Acts 17:28).

Take your singing to the next level and
share the Gospel message with confidence!

Since good music really cooks, why not try a self-help manual for singers filled with faith, humor, and easy-to-understand concert-tested recipes? **Cookin' Up a Song** by Carole Brewer will build your confidence with the secrets for effective breathing, beautiful tone quality, diction, stage presence, microphone and rehearsal techniques ...everything you want to know about singing plus more!

Available at Amazon.com

Thank you for telling others about Revitalize!

Have you been blessed by this book?
· *If so, please post a review on Amazon.com*

Other noteworthy sites:

○ **Be encouraged today! Visit Carole's blog at:**
http://carolebrewerministries.wordpress.com

Look for Carole Brewer speaking and music videos on YouTube

○ **Carole's Speaking & Music - Ministry clips**
https://youtu.be/X4CZa2CJluA

○ **Testimonials**
https://youtu.be/3cMxSlaFWJ4

○ **Voice of the Ocean – Wind Beneath My Wings**
https://www.youtube.com/watch?v=QBobsWUOkW4

CAROLE BREWER MINISTRIES
www.CaroleBrewer.com - www.BibleChicks.com
E. info@carolebrewer.com
PO Box 628, Fair Oaks, CA 95628

Carole Brewer

Made in the USA
San Bernardino, CA
14 January 2019